# THE ART OF CONNECTION™

## 365 Days of Abundance
## *Journaling*

**Robert W. Jones & Karen Clark-Reddon**
& The Authors of the Art of Connection

The Art of Connection – 365 Days of Abundance Journaling
Paperback ISBN: 978-1-965761-21-2

Spotlight Publishing House™ - Goodyear, AZ
https://spotlightpublishinghouse.com

Editor: Shawn M. Jones
Book Cover Design: Angie Ayala
Book Layout: Marigold2k

Robert W. Jones

Founder & Chairperson, Art of Connection, iNETrepreneur Network, Network Together, LLC.

Join us at an Event: https://business.inetrepreneurnetwork.com/events/calendar/

Set an Appointment: Discovery Session (koalendar.com)

Art of Connection Summit: https://artofconnectionsummit.com/

iNETrepreneur Magazine: http://inetrepreneurmagazine.com/

iNETrepreneur Radio: http://inetrepreneurradio.com/

Business Facebook: https://www.facebook.com/groups/businessreferralcommunity/

Instagram: https://www.instagram.com/inetrepreneur_network/

The common sunflower has a green erect stem covered in coarse hairs, growing on average around 2m tall. The leaves are broad, with serrated edges, and are alternately arranged on the stem. The 'flower' of the common sunflower is actually a pseudanthium, or flowerhead, made up of many small flowers.

-Royal Botanical Garden KEW

At the moment you think that you have lost everything, pause and remind yourself that you will always have everything you need and more!

-Karen Clark-Reddon

Date:_____

"*Just Hit Play!*"

_____

_____

_____

_____

_____

_____

_____

_____

_____

_____

_____

_____

_____

_____

_____

_____

_____

1

*- Sue Zee Finley*

"*True abundance is not just about wealth but the richness of purpose, compassion, and generosity that flows through our lives.*"

_____

_____

_____

_____

_____

_____

_____

_____

_____

_____

_____

_____

_____

_____

_____

_____

*- Laurel Pendle*

"True abundance is not measured by
what we possess but by our ability to
ensure that every member of our family
has a place to call home."

_____

_____

_____

_____

_____

_____

_____

_____

_____

_____

_____

_____

_____

_____

_____

_____

_____

- Raveen Arora

Date:_____

"*Live your when now!* "*When*" *may never come, but there's a now opportunity in every moment.*"

"May a deluge of abundance, victory, and joy wash away the inertia, lack, and unhappiness of your former self to enjoy an amazing life!"

- Vicky Melendez

Date:_____

*"Focus on the glimmers each day,
which are small moments that trigger
feelings of joy, calm, and safety."*

_____

_____

_____

_____

_____

_____

_____

_____

_____

_____

_____

_____

_____

_____

_____

_____

_____

*- Lauren Mazzoleni*

"*Talking and telling ain't training or selling*"

- David Doerrier

Date:_____

"To arrive at your oasis of abundance,
you will have to pursue your life purpose
with single-minded intent."

_____

_____

_____

_____

_____

_____

_____

_____

_____

_____

_____

_____

_____

_____

_____

_____

_____

_____

- Maggie Bellevue

Date:_____

"Abundance comes from the value you provide, not the qualities you have."

_____

_____

_____

_____

_____

_____

_____

_____

_____

_____

_____

_____

_____

_____

_____

_____

_____

- Jessica Moody

Date:_____

*"Crush inner demons; live in freedom!"*

_____
_____
_____
_____
_____
_____
_____
_____
_____
_____
_____
_____
_____
_____
_____
_____

*- Lilia Bogoeva*

Date:_____

"If I walk all the way through this lesson, I will receive permanent healing. Abundance comes from finishing lessons."

- Patricia Anderson

Date:_____

*"Time is your most significant factor in building financial security, so what money you keep and invest is more important than your annual income."*

Date:_____

"By ourselves, we can do amazing things, yet together, we can climb the highest mountain."

_____
_____
_____
_____
_____
_____
_____
_____
_____
_____
_____
_____
_____
_____
_____
_____
_____

- Mike Raber

Date:_____

"*Real change is an inside job; get the inside right, and the world will follow. Expect miracles along the way!*"

_____
_____
_____
_____
_____
_____
_____
_____
_____
_____
_____
_____
_____
_____
_____
_____
_____

- *Tara Pilling*

"Abundance, like a multifaceted diamond, shines in many forms: wealth, health, relationships, love, spirituality, and more."

- Nina V. Garza

Date:_____

"We are rich beyond measure. We are all trust fund babies, each of us heirs to this miraculous abundance called Life."

_____
_____
_____
_____
_____
_____
_____
_____
_____
_____
_____
_____
_____
_____
_____
_____
_____
_____

- Janet Vigil

*"Abundance has very little, if anything, to do with money. True abundance has to do with health and joy."*

*- Virginia Oman*

Date:_____

"There are generations of God's unborn children whose lives can be shaped by the moves you make, the things you say, and the actions you take forever!"

_____
_____
_____
_____
_____
_____
_____
_____
_____
_____
_____
_____
_____
_____
_____
_____
_____
_____
_____

- Bonnie Zaruches Lierse

Date:_____

"Rest is a right.
It is not something you earn!"

— Jenn Haston

Date:_____

"If you live in an abundance mentality, even through challenging times, the road becomes clear, and your connection with God becomes even stronger."

_____
_____
_____
_____
_____
_____
_____
_____
_____
_____
_____
_____
_____
_____
_____
_____
_____
_____

- Carol Koppelman

"*I have done too much work in the dark to lose in the light.*"

- Anthony Trucks

Date:_____

*"Stay aware of your deepest beliefs, for they drive or block your flow of abundance."*

"*You receive abundance at the level you are at, and abundance is infinite.*"

— *Preston Weekes*

Date:_____

"At least we're together!"

_____

_____

_____

_____

_____

_____

_____

_____

_____

_____

_____

_____

_____

_____

_____

_____

_____

Date:_____

"*Make the most of what you have
and take action from where
you are right now!*"

— Jennifer Capaldo

Date:_____

"When you challenge the borders of
your self-imposed box, you open yourself
up to a world of abundant possibilities
and boundless joys."

_____

_____

_____

_____

_____

_____

_____

_____

_____

_____

_____

_____

_____

_____

_____

_____

_____

- Anne Mayer

"*People who like to dream big help other people dream big.*"

---

---

---

---

---

---

---

---

---

---

---

---

---

---

---

*— Ira Koretsky*

Date:_____

"*Helping others win doesn't mean you lose... Instead, you'll multiply your wins.*"

- *Michael Lang*

"Live life like you're running
with scissors."

- Michael Fritzius

Date:_____

"Faith protects us from the unknown like a shield."

_____
_____
_____
_____
_____
_____
_____
_____
_____
_____
_____
_____
_____
_____
_____
_____

- Doug Giesler

*The name sunflower comes from the Greek words Helios meaning "sun" and Anthos meaning "flower".*

- Fair Oaks Farms

**Abundance unfolds when clarity and courage unite, inviting the world to respond to our true selves.**

- Shannon Morrison

Date:_____

"You're never too old, and it's never too late to change the direction of your life. You're one decision, one connection from your next opportunity!"

_____

_____

_____

_____

_____

_____

_____

_____

_____

_____

_____

_____

_____

_____

_____

_____

- Pamela Scott

"Decide what you want to be known for.
Every day, ask, 'How would the best
show up?' then, step up and do that."

- Candy Motzek

Date:_____

*"Live your life ambitiously now, and your future self will thank you."*

_____
_____
_____
_____
_____
_____
_____
_____
_____
_____
_____
_____
_____
_____
_____
_____
_____
_____

- Joellyn Wlazlowski Martin

"*You don't need to know the 'how' - just share your dream and let the connections guide you.*"

*- Becca Heissel*

Date:_____

"Never wish your life away – a life fully lived is a fulfilled life."

_____

_____

_____

_____

_____

_____

_____

_____

_____

_____

_____

_____

_____

_____

_____

_____

_____

_____

- Bonnie Verrico

Date:_____

"*Abundance, much like success, is something that must be defined and assessed by the individual seeking it.*"

— Rich Parsons

Date:_____

"Is that all you got? My abundance
stems from a lifetime of experiences."

_____

_____

_____

_____

_____

_____

_____

_____

_____

_____

_____

_____

_____

_____

_____

_____

_____

- Kenneth Hill, Jr.

Date:_____

*"The primary basis for the entire preeminence strategy is a keen commitment to empathy."*

*– Jay Abraham*

Date:_____

"Abundance comes when we trust God,
letting faith guide us through darkness and
transform pain into purpose, revealing life's
true richness."

- Marilyn Richards

40

"Abundance is not just about what we have but what we're willing to see in every moment."

- Christine Hiebel

Date:_____

"When we let go of the illusion we can control anything outside of us, we open the door to reclaiming our power and aligning with our authentic selves."

"Abundance is not the number of possessions you own. Abundance is who you have in your life and how you live your life. Abundance is your mindset."

_____

_____

_____

_____

_____

_____

_____

_____

_____

_____

_____

_____

_____

_____

_____

- Kathleen Edinger

Date:_____

*"Don't be so busy counting your steps
each day that you forget to notice the
abundance that surrounds you!
Stop and smell the roses!"*

_____
_____
_____
_____
_____
_____
_____
_____
_____
_____
_____
_____
_____
_____
_____
_____
_____
_____

*- Teresa Cundiff*

"Abundance isn't something you chase. It's something you become. Align with the frequency of abundance, and everything you desire flows into your life."

- Sherry Gideons

Date:_____

"To experience abundance requires serving others out of love with no expectations. It is the overflow of God's provisions and our contentment."

- J. Robert Santana

"Abundance is not just about having more, but it is about appreciating the right now to attract more than your eyes can see."

_____

_____

_____

_____

_____

_____

_____

_____

_____

_____

_____

_____

_____

_____

_____

_____

_____

*- Ashley Whitlock*

Date:_____

"Abundance isn't just about more for some;
it's about enough for all."

_____
_____
_____
_____
_____
_____
_____
_____
_____
_____
_____
_____
_____
_____
_____
_____
_____

- Lloyd Heath

"Our lives become more meaningful when we recognize the impact of our work on others. By humanizing the workplace, we empower positive change."

– Mika Cross

Date:_____

"Abundance is not about cash flow but rather resources money can't buy."

_____

_____

_____

_____

_____

_____

_____

_____

_____

_____

_____

_____

_____

_____

_____

_____

_____

- Nefertiti San Miguel

"There are two sides to every story, and when it comes to abundance, the sides are polar opposites."

_____

_____

_____

_____

_____

_____

_____

_____

_____

_____

_____

_____

_____

_____

_____

_____

_____

- Jacquelin Kenny

Date:_____

*"Success is built on the pillars of tools, systems, and leadership and leads to abundance."*

_____

_____

_____

_____

_____

_____

_____

_____

_____

_____

_____

_____

_____

_____

_____

_____

- D J Barton

"*Imagine the world you want to live in and step into you.*"

- *Katherine Kim Mullin*

Date:_____

"*Abundance is the essence of the soul's presence.*"

_____
_____
_____
_____
_____
_____
_____
_____
_____
_____
_____
_____
_____
_____
_____
_____
_____

"Consistently great client experiences are
created by repeating thoughtful actions
that have become systematized, not through
accidental encounters."

- Katie Evans

Date:_____

"When you are a giver, and you are open to receive, you will magnetically attract all the abundance your heart desires."

_____
_____
_____
_____
_____
_____
_____
_____
_____
_____
_____
_____
_____
_____
_____
_____
_____
_____

- Marla Press

Date:_____

"*Abundance is easy. Focusing on what you actually want is the tricky bit.*"

- *Catryn Becker*

Date:_____

"Symbols often have deep meanings
that can influence how we see the world
and ourselves."

- Michelle Snyder

Date:_____

"Instead of saying I have to or
I need to, my mantra is I get to."

-Laurissa Krishock

Date:_____

"The only worthwhile abundance to be cherished in your life is the multitude of other people you have helped enjoy more productive and happier lives."

_____

_____

_____

_____

_____

_____

_____

_____

_____

_____

_____

_____

_____

_____

_____

_____

_____

- Denise Meridith

"The intentional, consistent practice of expressing gratitude breathes life into our hopes, dreams, and aspirations."

- Traicey Finder

*Sunflowers are native to the Americas and were cultivated by indigenous tribes as early as 3000 BCE.*

- The Bouqs Co

When our forefathers fought for our Independence, they created a land of opportunity and abundance. The most important is the abundance of freedom.

- *John Verrico*

Date:_____

"Abundance is so much more than what
you have; it's a state of mind."

- Lori Osborne

Date:_____

"God is omnipotent (abundant), and
God is love; therefore, love is abundant,
so Abundance is the truth."

- David Waltzer

Date:_____

"Love was designed to be a forever emotion,
so why has yours, all of a sudden,
stopped?"

- Gene-O Cole

Date:_____

"Abundance happens in a moment!"

_____

_____

_____

_____

_____

_____

_____

_____

_____

_____

_____

_____

_____

_____

_____

_____

_____

"Cherish the abundance in your life,
whether it be health, wealth, family, or love.
For you are only here for a moment—
make it count."

- Sarren Scribner

Date:_____

"We invite abundance when we approach
life with an open mind and let go of
worries about scarcity."

_____
_____
_____
_____
_____
_____
_____
_____
_____
_____
_____
_____
_____
_____
_____
_____
_____
_____

- Yanick Sêïde

Date:_____

"Celebrating International Women's Day honors those who paved the way, giving us hope and strength to move forward through challenges and triumphs."

- Patty Hedrick

Date:_____

"Stop chasing the shiny objects in life
when you can apply polish to the
dull spots."

_____

_____

_____

_____

_____

_____

_____

_____

_____

_____

_____

_____

_____

_____

_____

_____

_____

- Michael Noyes

"You are the treasure that you are seeking."

- Rani Thanacoody

"Abundance is that quiet confidence you
show in life that helps pave your
life journey."

_____

_____

_____

_____

_____

_____

_____

_____

_____

_____

_____

_____

_____

_____

_____

_____

_____

- Vickie Gowdy

*"Your Legacy is something you live now, not just leave someday!"*

*– Joe Lander*

Date:_____

"Abundance is all around us;
all you have to do is look."

_____

_____

_____

_____

_____

_____

_____

_____

_____

_____

_____

_____

_____

_____

_____

_____

- Joanne Salvador

"*Your past may have shaped you,*
*but your past does not define your future*
*and who you are.*"

_____

_____

_____

_____

_____

_____

_____

_____

_____

_____

_____

_____

_____

_____

_____

*- Maria Mantoudakis*

Date:_____

*"Empowering your decisions with clarity and confidence in your finances is what I hope to help every business achieve."*

_____

_____

_____

_____

_____

_____

_____

_____

_____

_____

_____

_____

_____

_____

_____

_____

_____

_____

- Caroline Passmore

*"Love in abundance is the greatest treasure,*
*always closer than we think: in every smile,*
*hug, and compliment, the greatest*
*of God's gifts."*

_____

_____

_____

_____

_____

_____

_____

_____

_____

_____

_____

_____

_____

_____

_____

_____

_____

_____

*- Christine Kipp*

Date:_____

*"You are forever lost to the energy
of abundance if you only view it in
terms of money."*

_____

_____

_____

_____

_____

_____

_____

_____

_____

_____

_____

_____

_____

_____

_____

_____

_____

- *Kelly Hull Aho*

Date:_____

"Abundance of health is the greatest gift
one can possess; it's the foundation of
happiness that everyone aspires to be.
Health creates abundance."

- Soojin Kim

Date:_____

"The abundance you have in your life is reflective of how you love and prioritize yourself."

_____

_____

_____

_____

_____

_____

_____

_____

_____

_____

_____

_____

_____

_____

_____

_____

_____

- Heather Eileen Harris

"Stop... Focus... wherever you were,
wherever you are, you can always go...
where you want to be!"

— Carla Jansen Van Rosendaal

Date:_____

*"You already hold all the answers within. Trust your inner voice that guides you on the unique path that life has laid out for you."*

_____

_____

_____

_____

_____

_____

_____

_____

_____

_____

_____

_____

_____

_____

_____

_____

_____

- Angelika O'Rourke

Date:_____

"Emotions feel good for a moment.
Logic molds your life."

- Brian Swanson

Date:_____

"With Spirit, we unlock the most genuine power of abundance, not in what we own but in the undeniable truth that love and connection are eternal."

- Scott Allan

"If you keep doing what you're doing,
you're going to keep getting
what you got."

_____

_____

_____

_____

_____

_____

_____

_____

_____

_____

_____

_____

_____

_____

_____

_____

- Theresa Russell

Date:_____

"The vibrations of your words are sent
into the universe, which seeks out matching
vibrations (positive or negative), returning to
create your reality."

- Glenda Roberts

"*Learning can be effortless and abundant.*"

– Tonya Swainston

Date:_____

"I am at peace.
I know it will be okay."

_____

_____

_____

_____

_____

_____

_____

_____

_____

_____

_____

_____

_____

_____

_____

_____

- Paul Weigel

Date:_____

"You are the treasure that you
have been seeking."

_____
_____
_____
_____
_____
_____
_____
_____
_____
_____
_____
_____
_____
_____
_____
_____
_____

- Rani Thanacoody

Date:_____

"A mindset of abundance promotes
creativity, innovation, and transformation."

_____
_____
_____
_____
_____
_____
_____
_____
_____
_____
_____
_____
_____
_____
_____
_____
_____
_____

- Grace Gwitira

"Comparison builds walls against abundance, but giving crumbles those walls down."

_____
_____
_____
_____
_____
_____
_____
_____
_____
_____
_____
_____
_____
_____
_____
_____
_____

- Joseph Chipokosa

A single sunflower head can contain 1,000 to 2,000 seeds. The most common type of sunflower seed for snacking has a black-and-white striped hull.

-How Stuff Works

**Abundance is many things,
but it must be a mindset first!**

-Buddy Thornton

"*Relish in the gift of abundance.*"

- Ella Pahopin

Date:_____

"Intentional living is the bridge between where you are and where you want to be, built with the bricks of your strengths."

*"Facing death sharpens one's values, revealing what truly matters. Reclaim your strength and live your life fully, no matter the odds."*

*- Vanessa Abraham*

Date:_____

"Embracing your authenticity
can increase the abundance of peace
in your life."

_____

_____

_____

_____

_____

_____

_____

_____

_____

_____

_____

_____

_____

_____

_____

_____

_____

- Regina Spencer

Date:_____

"The abundance you desire already exists. You may not recognize it in its current form. Be willing to open your eyes, receive it, and give thanks."

_____

_____

_____

_____

_____

_____

_____

_____

_____

_____

_____

_____

_____

_____

_____

_____

_____

*- Michelle Carlen*

Date:_____

*"Behavioral clarity creates a path to an abundant reality."*

_____
_____
_____
_____
_____
_____
_____
_____
_____
_____
_____
_____
_____
_____
_____
_____
_____

- Kenyatta Turner

Date:_____

"Do what you love now,
and don't let your dreams pass you by."

– Jesse Orlando

Date:_____

"An abundance of abundance.
Can it be?"

_____
_____
_____
_____
_____
_____
_____
_____
_____
_____
_____
_____
_____
_____
_____
_____
_____

- Melissa Geracimos

Date:_____

"Embrace the unknown;
abundance lies beyond the door."

- Cynthia Beckles

Date:_____

*"As we perfect our habits of life, illness will become impossibly impossible."*

_____

_____

_____

_____

_____

_____

_____

_____

_____

_____

_____

_____

_____

_____

_____

_____

_____

_____

- *Sal Cavaliere*

Date:_____

"Understanding emotional resources
is the heartbeat of mental health, nourishing
connections that empower healing and
inspire resilience."

103

- Rahul K. Maharaj

Date:_____

"*Healing begins when we let go
of what no longer serves us rather than
stuff it within.*"

"Abundance is not measured by what we hold in our hands but by the infinite energy we hold in our hearts. Tune into this energy; the universe responds."

- Lisa Van Roode

Date:_____

"Abundance isn't just about having more;
it's about sharing what you have, knowing
that every act of kindness plants seeds for
future growth."

_____

_____

_____

_____

_____

_____

_____

_____

_____

_____

_____

_____

_____

_____

_____

_____

_____

- Maureen Ranks

"*Abundance does not equate to the number of material items you own but to the number of individuals who you love and reciprocate that love to you.*"

- Lisa E. Gongaware

Date:_____

"Do your best and just be you."

_____
_____
_____
_____
_____
_____
_____
_____
_____
_____
_____
_____
_____
_____
_____
_____
_____
_____

- Suzanne Söderberg

"Abundance is the art of seeing the beauty in simplicity; cherish the little things with gratitude, and life will reveal its infinite treasures."

– Eric Ranks

Date:_____

*"Don't let the world feed you the feeling of needing 'more' to live a full and abundant life; instead, take a step back and see that you are living it."*

_____

_____

_____

_____

_____

_____

_____

_____

_____

_____

_____

_____

_____

_____

_____

_____

_____

*- Anyssa Figueroa*

*"My beliefs dictate my behavior, and my behavior creates exceeding abundance."*

*- Marion Hill*

Date:_____

"*What you want already wants you,
and you are destined to have it!*"

_____
_____
_____
_____
_____
_____
_____
_____
_____
_____
_____
_____
_____
_____
_____
_____
_____
_____

*- Tammy De Mirza Lawing*

"Strength isn't built during comfort, but rising after life hits you hard. True resilience is shaped when we face challenges with grace and purpose."

- Brian Hawkins

Date:_____

"H.O.P.E can be an acronym for heck over pleasing everyone to hold on pain ends."

_____

_____

_____

_____

_____

_____

_____

_____

_____

_____

_____

_____

_____

_____

_____

_____

- Christa Rose

Date:_____

"Abundance isn't something to hope for.
It's all around you and within you every
moment of every day."

- Cindy Edington

"You try really hard to see images in clouds only others see, so share the same ideologies with others; perspectives; do."

- Denzel Smalls

"Small hands can make big waves."

- Miles Murdocca

Date:_____

"Through the sacrifices of those who came before us, we are reminded of the abundance of freedom, opportunity, and connection that surrounds us."

- Nicola Smith

"*Big dreams require a big heart. It requires exceptional perseverance. It requires that we never give up regardless of the obstacles we face.*"

*– Jeff Villwock*

Date:_____

*"Through my lens, I see an abundance of beauty and emotion. With photos, we freeze moments in time to create a wealth of memories that live on forever."*

- Denise Ackerman

"*It is never too late to heal your heart.*"

- David Brinker

*Sunflowers are not always yellow, and can also be red and purple.*

Earth Sky

**Symbols often have deep meanings that can influence how we see the world and ourselves.**

*- Michelle Snyder*

Date:_____

"Abundance is believing both:
"I have enough" and "there's more than
enough for everyone"."

- Chris Coraggio

Date:_____

"Don't have competitors. Have referral partners, confidants, and friends instead."

_Ann Brennan_

Date:_____

"*Abundance is the richness of relationships, belly laughs with friends, and serving others; it's every moment of every day of your life.*"

- *Karen Trapane*

Date:_____

_____
_____
_____
_____
_____
_____
_____
_____
_____
_____
_____
_____
_____
_____
_____
_____
_____

- Lori Osborne

"Any time I fail to see abundance in my life, it simply is because I am not looking."

_____

_____

_____

_____

_____

_____

_____

_____

_____

_____

_____

_____

_____

_____

_____

_____

_____

- Carrie Mosley

Date:_____

*"Living an abundant life starts with finding what fills your soul, training your mind, and recognizing joy in the tiniest moments of life."*

- Jessica Jorgensen

"Abundance is the cultivation of all
high vibrational things."

- Robert W. Jones

Date:_____

"*Reflect on the past, enjoy the present,
plan for the future.*"

- *Joseph Fang*

"An abundant mind finds value in time.
Uncovers moments of treasures sublime.
You choose the lenses you use to see.
How you react shapes who you'll be."

– Christina Christy Kruse

Date:_____

*"To make a difference without knowing
is the gift of life."*

_____
_____
_____
_____
_____
_____
_____
_____
_____
_____
_____
_____
_____
_____
_____
_____
_____

*- Andrew Elliman*

"Abundance is joy and sorrow in equal parts
made alive by imagination and
reason, enabling understanding, healing,
and partnership."

- Lila Bakke

Date:_____

*"You can attain a more abundant life when you allow yourself and others to naturally and safely release negative emotions."*

_____
_____
_____
_____
_____
_____
_____
_____
_____
_____
_____
_____
_____
_____
_____
_____
_____
_____
_____

*- Drina Fried*

Date:_____

*"When your life radiates contentment, you have achieved abundance, regardless of your circumstances."*

- *Marylou Leonard*

Date:_____

"*Abundance is HOPE:*
*helping other people everyday!*"

_____
_____
_____
_____
_____
_____
_____
_____
_____
_____
_____
_____
_____
_____
_____
_____
_____
_____

- Ken Greene

"Real transformation takes place in people's hearts, one person at a time."

- Mary Zennett

Date:_____

"Gratitude helps me see the abundance
in life and celebrate every day."

_____
_____
_____
_____
_____
_____
_____
_____
_____
_____
_____
_____
_____
_____
_____
_____

- Nancy Nance

Date:_____

"Bring your vision and light into
the world. Believe in the beauty
of your dreams."

– Barbara Goodman

Date:_____

"Abundance flourishes in the quiet
moments we share; a memory, a touch,
and a laugh together can fill
our hearts immensely."

_____
_____
_____
_____
_____
_____
_____
_____
_____
_____
_____
_____
_____
_____
_____
_____

- Amy D. Spring

"Plan the next 100 years, and you will know what you are going to do with your life today."

- Yvonne E. Gamble

Date:_____

"*Embrace the power within you to shape your reality. This reality is your life, too - it gets you to look, feel, and be however you want. You get to choose!*"

"Get intentional with abundance and Feng Shui... it's a conscious choice that turns intentions into reality."

_____
_____
_____
_____
_____
_____
_____
_____
_____
_____
_____
_____
_____
_____
_____
_____
_____

*- Maria Matias*

"*Influencers have fame and fortune,
but true power lies in shining your light
through the shadows cast by haters.*"

_____

_____

_____

_____

_____

_____

_____

_____

_____

_____

_____

_____

_____

_____

_____

_____

_____

*- Brenda Kilhoffer*

"Never underestimate those you meet;
everyone has a story to tell. Genuine
connections, built on trust,
will always prevail."

- Jim Connors (JC)

Date:_____

"*Physical health is achievable,*
*but it must be integrated with mental,*
*emotional, and spiritual health.*"

_____
_____
_____
_____
_____
_____
_____
_____
_____
_____
_____
_____
_____
_____
_____
_____
_____

- Vincent Leonti

"We can all focus on being creative. It's research, risking & making. At that moment, you forget everything. Your senses engage, and you just make."

- Monika Jakubiak

Date:_____

"*Shining brightly with abundance!*"

_____

_____

_____

_____

_____

_____

_____

_____

_____

_____

_____

_____

_____

_____

_____

_____

*- Howard Brown*

"Abundance is all around us; the Law of Attraction demonstrates abundance daily!"

- Kevin Mayer

*Sunflowers can range in height, from dwarf varieties that are less than two feet tall to the world's tallest sunflower at 30 feet and 1 inch.*

-National Sunflower Association

**Abundance is so much more than what you have; it's a state of mind.**

*Lori Osborne*

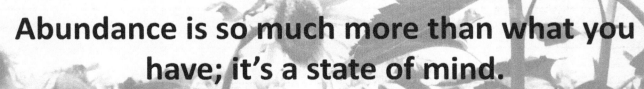

"*Doing what you love and loving what you do unlocks true abundance.*"

_____

_____

_____

_____

_____

_____

_____

_____

_____

_____

_____

_____

_____

_____

_____

_____

_____

*- Karsten Alva- Jorgensen*

Date:_____

"*Abundance is not a destination to be sought but is a place you come from - it's a state of mind.*"

"Every moment of indecision is a choice,
but abundance flows through
decisive action."

- Hannah Kesler

Date:_____

"You are the only you, so go be the best
you that you can be!"

_____
_____
_____
_____
_____
_____
_____
_____
_____
_____
_____
_____
_____
_____
_____
_____
_____
_____

"Abundance is a frequency that you
have to magnetize."

- Brenda Thanacoody

Date:_____

*"Finding my people made a difference in my life and taught me how to make a difference in others."*

_____

_____

_____

_____

_____

_____

_____

_____

_____

_____

_____

_____

_____

_____

_____

_____

*- Barb Markey*

Date:_____

*"You get to define abundance in all areas of life, and when you feel it, really feel it, you get to live it."*

157

*— Kathleen Carlson*

Date:_____

"You can grow old in numbers
but never grow up in your heart."

_____

_____

_____

_____

_____

_____

_____

_____

_____

_____

_____

_____

_____

_____

_____

_____

_____

- Tonni Lea Larson

"Never underestimate simply showing up with a golden energy and a curious mind!"

_____

_____

_____

_____

_____

_____

_____

_____

_____

_____

_____

_____

_____

_____

_____

_____

_____

_____

_____

- Holly Enzmann

"Has someone ever said to you,
"Just do it?" "What are you waiting
for?" "Go for it!""

_____
_____
_____
_____
_____
_____
_____
_____
_____
_____
_____
_____
_____
_____
_____
_____
_____
_____

- Michelle Gass

Date:_____

"Envision the end, not the beginning."

- Roy Moore

Date:_____

"*True abundance is found in inner happiness, peace of mind, grace, self-worth, and a grateful heart.*"

_____

_____

_____

_____

_____

_____

_____

_____

_____

_____

_____

_____

_____

_____

_____

_____

_____

- Becky Norwood

"Living a life full of abundance is
soothing for the soul."

- Tres Chapman

Date:_____

"Ignite your sparkle...your soul is
meant to shine."

_____
_____
_____
_____
_____
_____
_____
_____
_____
_____
_____
_____
_____
_____
_____
_____

- Bobbi Wilcox

"Sometimes, too much is what you need."

- K.M. Ringer

Date:_____

"In the dance of life, open your awareness
to the beauty that surrounds us every day.
Embrace it with an abundance of gratitude.
Live life full force."

- Jodie Santandrea-Ruano

Date:_____

*"Who kares, we care!!*
*Creating change, one life at a time!!"*

_____
_____
_____
_____
_____
_____
_____
_____
_____
_____
_____
_____
_____
_____
_____
_____

*– Todd Lingel*

Date:_____

"Evolving ideas, one conversation
at a time."

_____

_____

_____

_____

_____

_____

_____

_____

_____

_____

_____

_____

_____

_____

_____

_____

- Kevin McDonald

*"Abundance is an inside job.*
*No one can take that away from you."*

- *Wendy B. King*

Date:_____

"Tomorrow is my favorite day because I'll be alive to enjoy it."

_____
_____
_____
_____
_____
_____
_____
_____
_____
_____
_____
_____
_____
_____
_____
_____
_____
_____
_____

Date:_____

*"An abundant mindset on a foundation of integrity fueled by God will give you a journey of impact and service."*

_____
_____
_____
_____
_____
_____
_____
_____
_____
_____
_____
_____
_____
_____
_____
_____

*— Ken Rochon*

Date:_____

"Abundance is sharing family, connection, and life experiences with others."

_____
_____
_____
_____
_____
_____
_____
_____
_____
_____
_____
_____
_____
_____
_____
_____
_____

- James Edinger

"There are no bad people, only the unconscious - those who are asleep, living in patterns, conditioned to play roles in dreams that are not their own."

- Andreea Parc

Date:_____

"True abundance is creating purpose,
uplifting others, and sharing success—
because when we help others grow,
we all thrive."

_____

_____

_____

_____

_____

_____

_____

_____

_____

_____

_____

_____

_____

_____

_____

_____

- Craig Darling

"Abundance unfolds when clarity and courage unite, inviting the world to respond to our true selves."

— Shannon Morrison

"When you release the things you hold so tightly, it allows you to open your hand to receive."

_— Melody Vachal_

"Fulfillment comes from a state of being, not having – it's embracing the divine flow of life and knowing that everything needed is already within."

– Mary Van Alstyne

Date:_____

"Financial abundance is built on faith.
Trust the journey, embrace the promises,
and see how belief turns challenges into
prosperous opportunities."

- Joseph Blake, Jr.

178

*In 2012, U.S. astronaut Don Pettit brought sunflower seeds to the International Space Station.*

-Space.com

**If I walk all the way through this lesson, I will receive permanent healing. Abundance comes from finishing lessons.**

*- Patricia Anderson*

Date:_____

"*Abundance is akin to a shapeshifter, as both entities bring blessings in multiple forms.*"

_____
_____
_____
_____
_____
_____
_____
_____
_____
_____
_____
_____
_____
_____
_____
_____
_____
_____

- Barbara Hazelden

Date:_____

"Emptiness is the beginning
of abundance."

181

— Jennie James

Date:_____

"*Every decision is an investment in our business, personal abundance, and the legacy of prosperity we create.*"

Date:_____

*"For me, connection has always meant having the courage to show up authentically as I am, flaws and all, and creating space for others to do the same."*

*- Amber Golden*

Date:_____

"To all people who have fallen victim to abuse as children and never had a voice to speak up. I hear you, and I am with you because I am you."

Date:_____

"It's not the fortune we accumulate but
the love we share that defines us;
every act of kindness creates ripples with the
ability to transform lives."

- Deidre Lopez

Date:_____

"A diagnosis of Parkinson's disease
may not mean the beginning of the end -
it could be the start of the most rewarding
period of your life."

_____

_____

_____

_____

_____

_____

_____

_____

_____

_____

_____

_____

_____

_____

_____

_____

_____

- Larry Linton

Date:_____

"We're all storytellers and creators.
The stories we tell ourselves, good or bad,
are the foundation of the destiny we're in the
process of creating."

- Daniel Pedemonte

Date:_____

"Abundance flows when trust is cultivated - acts of integrity, transparency, and connection sow the seeds of opportunity and lasting collaboration."

- Jeffrey Morris

"*Abundance appears after we fully and freely give to others, and then it comes to stay.*"

*- Ginny Correa-Creager*

Date:_____

*"The objective of life isn't about trying to get through the ride without getting thrown; it's about how quickly we can get back on after being thrown."*

_____

_____

_____

_____

_____

_____

_____

_____

_____

_____

_____

_____

_____

_____

_____

_____

_____

- *Cowboy Joe Marques*

"When our forefathers fought for our Independence, they created a land of opportunity and abundance. The most important is the abundance of freedom."

191                                                    – John Verrico

Date:_____

"The feeling of abundance is a feeling
that makes your buns wanna dance!"

_____

_____

_____

_____

_____

_____

_____

_____

_____

_____

_____

_____

_____

_____

_____

_____

_____

- Julie D'Ann

"The abundance of a mother's love for her children can never be diminished! It is an unbreakable connection and a lasting presence – even beyond life."

– LaBarbara Dhaliwal

Date:_____

"Creating with the infinite - abundance
multiplies right where our attention lies."

_____
_____
_____
_____
_____
_____
_____
_____
_____
_____
_____
_____
_____
_____
_____
_____
_____

- Brett Cotter

"Abundance simply means " a lot of.""

- Jennifer Farrar

Date:_____

*"Abundance is created through living your life's purpose."*

- Tawni Acosta

"Change is inevitable;
growth is intentional."

– Samuel Knickerbocker

Date:_____

"Abundance is a force-field of
resilience superpower."

― J. Lumen

Date:_____

"*True abundance is emotional freedom, the courage to shed what no longer serves us and embrace what brings us pure joy!*"

199

*- Suzi Freeman*

"When your heart calls, answer it.
Be your best you by honoring your
own heart and giving of your
heart abundantly."

_____

_____

_____

_____

_____

_____

_____

_____

_____

_____

_____

_____

_____

_____

_____

_____

_____

- Becky Estby

"Abundance: God's perspective."

- Corina Blake

"*I'm open to the possibility that...*"

_____
_____
_____
_____
_____
_____
_____
_____
_____
_____
_____
_____
_____
_____
_____
_____

"If you have a roof over your head, a
fridge with food, clothes to wear, a person
to hug, and a caring community,
you have all the riches on earth."

- Yousef Qabazard

Date:_____

"*Abundance is not a glass half empty or half full. Abundance is the glass is always full.*"

_____

_____

_____

_____

_____

_____

_____

_____

_____

_____

_____

_____

_____

_____

_____

_____

_____

- Ophir Adar

Date:_____

"Trusting the Creator's perfect timing.
I'm unique, made to share joy and
abundance with every breath. This trust is
for you, too, when you choose it!"

- Daniel Simon

"Stop thinking about negative thoughts; they are more powerful in magnitude than positive thinking for removing the barriers to achieving your goals."

- Troy Hipolito

Date:_____

"Contained within the structure of abundance is your unique energy-print of brilliance; your creational potential awaits."

- Laura Ballet

*Sunflowers are Ukraine's national flower.*
-Blossoming Gifts

A book isn't just words on a page – it's your
legacy, a story that will live on long after you've
written the final chapter.

-Mattie Murrey

"The blessings found in everyday
life multiplied by the joy found in
each one can create abundance beyond
your wildest dreams."

— Elisabeth Garner

Date:_____

"*Abundance is found in the love and wisdom we share; we create ripples of legacy that last forever.*"

_____

_____

_____

_____

_____

_____

_____

_____

_____

_____

_____

_____

_____

_____

_____

_____

_____

- Natalie McQueen

"Like sunshine breaking through night, we can rise from darkness, embrace our potential, and light up the world around us."

- Shirley Turner

Date:_____

"We possess all we need by having
a colorful abundance of heart, mind,
body, and soul."

_____
_____
_____
_____
_____
_____
_____
_____
_____
_____
_____
_____
_____
_____
_____
_____
_____

- Linda MacDougall

Date:_____

"The secret to abundance?
Appreciate the present, and the future
unfolds with greater gifts."

- Jana Short

Date:_____

*"Life is a hike; No two hikes turn out exactly the same because of the paths you choose."*

_____
_____
_____
_____
_____
_____
_____
_____
_____
_____
_____
_____
_____
_____
_____
_____
_____
_____

- Rebecca Babcock

"Abundance is built on strong, transparent relationships, collaboration, fun, and creating lasting memories together."

_____

_____

_____

_____

_____

_____

_____

_____

_____

_____

_____

_____

_____

_____

_____

_____

_____

_____

- Doris Lum

Date:_____

*"The questions you ask yourself shape the path to your potential."*

_____

_____

_____

_____

_____

_____

_____

_____

_____

_____

_____

_____

_____

_____

_____

_____

- Sylvia Baffour

Date:_____

"Creating a lasting impression on the world and those around you involves having a family legacy."

- Debbie Steagall

Date:_____

"We build a better world by connecting.
Connecting with ourselves, with the
world's realities, and possibilities, and with
others on the same quest."

- Sarah Clark

"*You are just one connection away from meeting your golden connection!*"

*- Daniel Knight*

"Abundance is a constant, and it reveals its true magic when it flows from a life well-lived."

_____

_____

_____

_____

_____

_____

_____

_____

_____

_____

_____

_____

_____

_____

_____

_____

_____

- Shawna James

"Endurance today leads to the
blessings of tomorrow."

- Erica Crouch

Date:_____

"Find the beauty or create it yourself."

_____
_____
_____
_____
_____
_____
_____
_____
_____
_____
_____
_____
_____
_____
_____
_____

- Jennifer Miller

Date:_____

*"An inspired choice today creates the change leading to your success story tomorrow."*

*- Caroline Biesalski*

*"True richness comes not from the belongings we own but from the cherished moments we experience and the connections we foster."*

― Leann Coakley

Date:_____

*"Live an inner-directed life, giving, doing, loving, serving, all from your abundance!"*

*– David Knepp*

Date:_____

"It isn't logical that world leaders have convinced the human race that it takes wars to bring back peace."

_____

_____

_____

_____

_____

_____

_____

_____

_____

_____

_____

_____

_____

_____

_____

_____

_____

- Lydia G. Fougères

"*The most successful wealth plans I've seen are, in no small part—escape plans.*"

- *Andy Tanner*

Date:_____

"Abundance flows through the connections
we cultivate. Every shared success
celebrated amplifies our growth and joy."

_____
_____
_____
_____
_____
_____
_____
_____
_____
_____
_____
_____
_____
_____
_____
_____
_____
_____

- Mary Gaul

Date:_____

"Intentional abundance is a
practiced mindset."

- Tricia Livermore

"If your why is big enough, you will
do anything; you will do everything!
"Dancing to my African drumbeat."

_____
_____
_____
_____
_____
_____
_____
_____
_____
_____
_____
_____
_____
_____
_____
_____
_____

- Sanet Van Breda

"*I see evidence of my alignment with my manifestation.*"

*- Naheed Oberfeld*

Date:_____

"*Abundance isn't chased; it's a state we embrace. Your journey today creates the richness of tomorrow and the joy of now.*"

_____

_____

_____

_____

_____

_____

_____

_____

_____

_____

_____

_____

_____

_____

_____

_____

_____

_____

- *Kristin Hannum*

"Soar with faith, and abundance
will follow."

- Susan Flerchinger

Date:_____

"Sharing your transformational Soul story offers hope to others."

_____

_____

_____

_____

_____

_____

_____

_____

_____

_____

_____

_____

_____

_____

_____

_____

- Mary E. Knippel

Date:_____

"The mind is limitlessly spacious and limitlessly powerful."

_____

_____

_____

_____

_____

_____

_____

_____

_____

_____

_____

_____

_____

_____

_____

_____

- Rachael Hudson

Date:_____

"Think about what is the
Greatest Abundance!"

_____
_____
_____
_____
_____
_____
_____
_____
_____
_____
_____
_____
_____
_____
_____
_____
_____

- Radavie Riom

"*If there is a gift attached to every pain you have, you should see the gift as a blessing in disguise!*"

*- Ching Fong Sin*

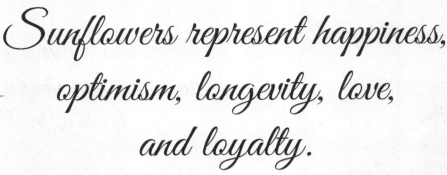

*Sunflowers represent happiness, optimism, longevity, love, and loyalty.*

-1800Flowers

**Best Kept Secrets on How to Pay for Senior Services.**

*-Therese Johnson*

"My life is so full of abundance that it overflows. I am in wonder at how this happens. I am "wonder... full.""

- Jaclyn Zoccoli

Date:_____

"*Life. Breath. Thought. Sight. Smell. Taste. Touch. A spark of all that is. You, Source/God/Goddess/Divine Spark, you are abundance!*"

- Audrey Kerger

Date:_____

*"Best kept secrets on how to pay for senior services."*

*- Therese Johnson*

Date:_____

*"Plant the seed- Nourish the stem-watch it bloom! And, of course, there's always room to flourish!"*

_____

_____

_____

_____

_____

_____

_____

_____

_____

_____

_____

_____

_____

_____

_____

_____

*- Mary J. Robinson*

*"The impact of volunteering for the community you are a part of will go beyond the time given. It transforms lives and creates lifetime connections."*

_____

_____

_____

_____

_____

_____

_____

_____

_____

_____

_____

_____

_____

_____

_____

_____

_____

*- Wesley Swainston*

Date:_____

"If people understood that happiness is a
skill, something we can practice and teach
our brains to do on command, the world
would change forever."

- Greg Goddard

"To build, you must first destroy."

- Tanner Seehausen

Date:_____

*"What I say makes my day,
and what I say can make or break
someone else's day!"*

_____

_____

_____

_____

_____

_____

_____

_____

_____

_____

_____

_____

_____

_____

_____

_____

*- Sherry Anshara*

"Hold the vision; trust the timing.
The course is already set."

247

- Nicola Smith

"*Don't let anyone tell you something about you that they don't know about themselves. They can't know who you are, for they don't know who they are.*"

_____
_____
_____
_____
_____
_____
_____
_____
_____
_____
_____
_____
_____
_____
_____
_____

- Rabea Katharina Stenger

"True strength is firm yet flexible."

- Clifford Starks

"Upgrading your mindset is like updating your software; an outdated mindset can't support the changes you need to level up in life."

_____
_____
_____
_____
_____
_____
_____
_____
_____
_____
_____
_____
_____
_____
_____
_____

- Althea Samuels

Date:_____

"The "how" is the story we will tell
afterward; it was never meant to be used to
look forward."

- Kara Atkinson

Date:_____

"*I am grateful for all the abundance that has already been given in the past, as well as the time yet to come.*"

_____

_____

_____

_____

_____

_____

_____

_____

_____

_____

_____

_____

_____

_____

_____

_____

- *Pat Young*

"The most powerful thing in the universe is mind clarity. Once we discover what we want, we need to commit to excellence and whatever it takes."

_____

_____

_____

_____

_____

_____

_____

_____

_____

_____

_____

_____

_____

_____

_____

*– Ira Rosen*

Date:_____

"Encouraging young people to do acts of
service and kindness will bring about an
abundance of joy and love into our world
for generations to come."

_____

_____

_____

_____

_____

_____

_____

_____

_____

_____

_____

_____

_____

_____

_____

_____

_____

- Kylah Waits

Date:_____

"*Acknowledgment gives voice and viability to another.*"

*- Laura Piel*

"Ditch food stress & scale drama!
Adulting = freedom
(even if you burn dinner)."

- Annie Deckert

Date:_____

"*Your birthright of abundance is in your DNA. Unlocking your unique access code will lead you to a life of abundance and success!*"

*- Crystal Turner*

"Abundance isn't something to chase;
it's something to uncover and share."

_____
_____
_____
_____
_____
_____
_____
_____
_____
_____
_____
_____
_____
_____
_____
_____

- Uchenna Faumuina-Eze

*"Dis-ease is not a sign that our bodies are broken but rather a nudge from our bodies to push us to live more in alignment with our true nature."*

— Tina Koopersmith

"We're all storytellers and creators. The stories we tell ourselves, good or bad, are the foundation of the destiny we're in the process of creating."

_____

_____

_____

_____

_____

_____

_____

_____

_____

_____

_____

_____

_____

_____

_____

_____

_____

- Daniel Pedemonte

"Think abundantly; don't allow limited thinking to change your mindset, as those who think abundantly have a better chance to attract a lot more."

_____

_____

_____

_____

_____

_____

_____

_____

_____

_____

_____

_____

_____

_____

_____

_____

_____

– Maurice Montoya

"We're all connected as humans first &
the bottom line begins with relationships -
how we choose to relate daily determines
what we create daily!"

- Maris Segal

Date:_____

"Abundance must be found in the heart
before it has meaning."

- Robert Thornton

Date:_____

"This day, this life - it's a gift.
That is why it's called the present."

_____

_____

_____

_____

_____

_____

_____

_____

_____

_____

_____

_____

_____

_____

_____

_____

- Char McCreadie

"A book isn't just words on a page – it's your legacy, a story that will live on long after you've written the final chapter."

- Mattie Murrey

*The seeds are a rich source of protein, potassium, magnesium, calcium, iron, and vitamin E. The seeds can be ground into flour or used to make oil.*

-Symbolic Meaning of a Flower

**Abundance shows up in many forms throughout life. It has been said that abundance is a state of plenty. A supply of whatever is desired.**

-Adrianne Size

"The definition and manifestation of abundance in one's life depends on the perspective of the one defining it."

_____

_____

_____

_____

_____

_____

_____

_____

_____

_____

_____

_____

_____

_____

_____

_____

_____

- Rizah Valdez

Date:_____

"Abundance isn't what you store;
it's about what you offer."

_____

_____

_____

_____

_____

_____

_____

_____

_____

_____

_____

_____

_____

_____

_____

_____

_____

- Ayden VanWie-Hamerla

Date:_____

"The quotation that I have submitted is my own and not from anyone else or any other source."

269

— Stuart Gethner

Date:_____

"*Abundance flows where gratitude and love meet, reminding us that everything we need is already within reach.*"

"The man who learns to embrace abundance will live a full life of experiences, relationships, and personal growth."

– Leonard DeCarmine

"Adjust and pivot to the changes around us, no matter the circumstances. Be willing to change our attitudes to embrace the growth that comes from it."

- Fernando Sanchez

"Every kind word contributes to the wellbeing and peace of us all, just as every plastic bag saved contributes to the well-being of our planet."

- Annette Dernick

"Today is my calling;
tomorrow is its reflection;
abundance is embedded within it."

_____

_____

_____

_____

_____

_____

_____

_____

_____

_____

_____

_____

_____

_____

_____

_____

_____

_____

- Myra Murphy

"With each exhale, release doubt;
with each inhale, allow for the infinite
possibility, and you will know that
abundance is who you genuinely are!"

- Deborah Kym

Date:_____

"*Infuse your life with abundance, and watch your happiness multiply!*"

_____

_____

_____

_____

_____

_____

_____

_____

_____

_____

_____

_____

_____

_____

_____

_____

_____

- Nathalie Botros

"Some will, some won't. So what, someone's waiting!"

- Nico Stringfellow

"It's all about love."

_____

_____

_____

_____

_____

_____

_____

_____

_____

_____

_____

_____

_____

_____

_____

_____

_____

- Satie Narain-Simon

Date:_____

*"One needs only to invest in others to realize true abundance."*

_____
_____
_____
_____
_____
_____
_____
_____
_____
_____
_____
_____
_____
_____
_____
_____

*- Kathi Hall*

Date:_____

"*Mindsets are static; life moves!*"

_____

_____

_____

_____

_____

_____

_____

_____

_____

_____

_____

_____

_____

_____

_____

_____

- Doug Giesler

Date:_____

"Abundance is a state of mind!"

- Debra Lee Murrow

Date:_____

"Months ago, GBS left me paralyzed in the ICU. Life's storms are fierce; faith and determination guide you, and you will sail through and rise again!"

- Gabriella Kipp

"True strength isn't in never falling. It's in rising, growing, and connecting with purpose every time you do."

- Gina Matteson

Date:_____

"Abundance is many things,
but it must be a mindset first!"

Date:_____

*"Warp speed your way to abundance:
Connect... Develop... Succeed...!"*

*- Colleen Strube*

Date:_____

"*Let's set sail for the stars –
it is pointless to wait.*"

---

---

---

---

---

---

---

---

---

---

---

---

---

---

---

---

---

*- Robert Enzmann*

"Feed your white wolf!"

- Ophir Adar

Date:_____

"Abundance is everywhere; it is not invisible;
we just have to be willing to see it."

_____
_____
_____
_____
_____
_____
_____
_____
_____
_____
_____
_____
_____
_____
_____
_____
_____

- Mayra Hawkins

"Sometimes, you just have to let things unfold."

- Melissa Geracimos

Date:_____

"To experience lack and be
gratefully content is the byproduct of
abundance in life!"

_____

_____

_____

_____

_____

_____

_____

_____

_____

_____

_____

_____

_____

_____

_____

_____

_____

- J. Robert Santana

Date:_____

"Discover your greatness through your biggest mistakes."

- Diana Hooker

"*Leaning into loving yourself through soul work will create recycled energy that you will be able to share abundantly with others.*"

— Dana Schon

"A life of abundance does not come
from material things but from God,
gratitude, and love."

- Georgette Combs

Date:_____

"It's not the happy people that are
grateful; it is the grateful people
that are happy."

_____

_____

_____

_____

_____

_____

_____

_____

_____

_____

_____

_____

_____

_____

_____

_____

_____

- Jeff Marconette, Jr.

*"True abundance is born from the courage to confront our deepest fears, unravel our subconscious beliefs, and transform pain into power."*

*- Tammy DeMirza Lawing*

Sunflowers have been utilized in phytoremediation efforts to extract toxic substances, such as lead, arsenic, and uranium, from contaminated soils. Notably, they were planted near the Chernobyl disaster site to assist in decontamination.

-She Said Sunflower

**Plan the next 100 years, and you will know what you are going to do with your life today.**

-Yvonne E. Gamble

"Expectations without agreement create premeditated resentment."

- Ken Ashby

Date:_____

"*Abundance is not about the material things you have; it's about the quality of the beautiful things that are in your life.*"

_____
_____
_____
_____
_____
_____
_____
_____
_____
_____
_____
_____
_____
_____
_____
_____
_____
_____
_____
_____

- Suzanne LaFlamme

"Abundance is only as calm and peaceful as you build it."

– Mishianand Mack

Date:_____

"Change is an emotional journey.
Change is uncomfortable. It forces you
to evaluate who you truly are.
The beauty is in the possibilities."

- Dr. Michelle Mras

"*Health is the cornerstone of abundance.*"

*- Laura Lee Kenny*

Date:_____

"Abundance is everywhere.
Wealth flows when you offer solutions
that enrich others' lives."

Date:_____

"Remember that happiness will never come from an abundance of possessions but through sharing your time and resources with others."

- Nathan Keller

Date:_____

"Dreamers fill their Bucket Lists;
Courageous souls empty them."

_____
_____
_____
_____
_____
_____
_____
_____
_____
_____
_____
_____
_____
_____
_____
_____

- Lauren Miller

"I have all the time I need to accomplish what I have been "called" to do in my life and all the things I "need" to get done in the meantime."

- Diana Ringer

Date:_____

"*Abundance is what happens in your life and business when you have no luck, but apply the Four Cs: Clarity - Courage - Confidence - Consistency.*"

- Alex Vitillo

Date:_____

*"To live abundantly is to train your mind,
body, emotions, and spirit to be healthy."*

*- Joanne Angel BarryColon*

Date:_____

"True abundance is not measured by what we gather but by what we give cheerfully and joyfully with compassion and empathy and the joy we find therein."

- Lana Stevenson

"It's not about all the "stuff"
you have been blessed with or acquired.
It's about the people with whom God
has graced your life."

*- Sherlyn Halloran*

Date:_____

"All is well in my peaceful and
prosperous world!"

"Overcoming today's struggles opens
doors to an abundance of wisdom
and opportunities."

_____

_____

_____

_____

_____

_____

_____

_____

_____

_____

_____

_____

_____

_____

_____

_____

_____

- Ro Gonzalez

Date:_____

*"The more you recognize your blessings, the more the universe expands them—only in sharing do they genuinely flourish."*

_____

_____

_____

_____

_____

_____

_____

_____

_____

_____

_____

_____

_____

_____

_____

_____

_____

*- Karla Garjaka*

*"True abundance flows when we accept life as it is —and as it isn't. By embracing reality without resistance, we open ourselves to all life has to offer."*

_____

_____

_____

_____

_____

_____

_____

_____

_____

_____

_____

_____

_____

_____

_____

_____

*- Heather Orlando*

Date:_____

*"Appreciation is the mother of abundance when you count your blessings, the number becomes infinite."*

_____
_____
_____
_____
_____
_____
_____
_____
_____
_____
_____
_____
_____
_____
_____
_____
_____
_____

- SueZee Finley

Date:_____

"My idea of abundance is nuts...
pistachios that is!"

315

- SueZee Finley

"Money, power, hope for a brighter future – all this is secondary. Live fully each day and find something that brings you joy, no matter how small."

- Andrew Paul Skoog

"Empower others; inspire growth.
Every person has the power to
make a difference!"

- Wendy Sellers

Date:_____

"The secret to life is to believe in yourself, pursue your passion, and never quit believing in making your dreams come true and soar!"

_____
_____
_____
_____
_____
_____
_____
_____
_____
_____
_____
_____
_____
_____
_____
_____

- Hank Longo

Date:_____

"An idea sparked by curiosity is the compass that lights the way to a life of abundance that can't be measured."

- Niurka Castaneda

Date:_____

"Time may be finite, yet love and
abundance are vast in possibilities."

_____
_____
_____
_____
_____
_____
_____
_____
_____
_____
_____
_____
_____
_____
_____
_____
_____

- Julie Jones

Date:_____

"*Life is not some splendid monument to be built but an unfolding adventure to be experienced.*"

- *Art Blanchford*

Date:_____

"Aligning with your heart and your true self is living in your light and serving at your best."

_____
_____
_____
_____
_____
_____
_____
_____
_____
_____
_____
_____
_____
_____
_____
_____

- Nancy Itokazu

"Daily gratitude is the key to
an abundant life."

- Sofia Pinky Magana

The tallest sunflower ever recorded reached 30 feet 1 inch (9.17 meters), cultivated by Hans-Peter Schiffer in Kaarst, Germany, in August 2014.

-Guinness World Records

My life is so full of abundance that it overflows. I am in wonder at how this happens. I am "wonder. . .full."

-Jaclyn Zoccoli

"We are born curious. We grow up to understand. We age to guide."

- Shad Hardy

Date:_____

*"You ultimately make your own choices in life. Dream big. Lean into God. Trust in happiness."*

- Laci Waddill

Date:_____

"There are symbiotic relationships between design, nature, and intention."

- Holly Berry

"You have to suit up and show up if you
want to stand up and speak up."

_____

_____

_____

_____

_____

_____

_____

_____

_____

_____

_____

_____

_____

_____

_____

_____

- Laura Cobb

"A life of abundance is living your spectacular vision with brilliance, drive, and absolute clarity."

- Bethany Newell

Date:_____

"Building connections in a blended family takes time. Be brave, communicate, and remember: love grows when we understand each other."

_____

_____

_____

_____

_____

_____

_____

_____

_____

_____

_____

_____

_____

_____

_____

_____

- Nyasha Hulse

Date:_____

"An angel mom loves beyond the ordinary, healing hearts with sacrifice. The light placed you to build a family and lasting change."

- Ruth Dorsainville-Hulse

Date:_____

*"It's not your fault;*
*it's your responsibility. This statement is*
*especially true as a husband and father*
*in a blended family."*

_____

_____

_____

_____

_____

_____

_____

_____

_____

_____

_____

_____

_____

_____

_____

- *Bruce Hulse*

"When we awaken to the abundance within us, we will naturally radiate abundance."

- Kimberly Yvonne Humphreys

Date:_____

"*Abundance is in your head;
you can think so that you can create.*"

_____

_____

_____

_____

_____

_____

_____

_____

_____

_____

_____

_____

_____

_____

_____

_____

_____

- Yvonne Schimmel

Date:_____

"I don't need to blow out your candle to make mine burn brighter. Together, our combined light can help each other eliminate the darkness for all."

335

— John Verrico

Date:_____

"Often, we think we know the problem, but true leadership requires us to dig deeper; to turn overwhelm into opportunity and burnout into brilliance."

"Abundance is within you; it awakens when your imagination dares to believe beyond what your eyes can perceive."

_____

_____

_____

_____

_____

_____

_____

_____

_____

_____

_____

_____

_____

_____

_____

_____

– Martina Wagner

Date:_____

"In loss, connection becomes our lifeline—
a bridge from solitude to shared strength."

_____
_____
_____
_____
_____
_____
_____
_____
_____
_____
_____
_____
_____
_____
_____
_____
_____

- Lynn Banis

Date:_____

"*Live your Legacy while you Build it!*"

339

*- Lady Jen Du Plessis*

Date:_____

_____
_____
_____
_____
_____
_____
_____
_____
_____
_____
_____
_____
_____
_____
_____
_____

- David Doerrier

"True Abundance is the ability to dream so big that you can include others; dreams in it!"

- Mamie- Jean Lamley

Date:_____

"*Positive speaking gets them listening!*"

_____

_____

_____

_____

_____

_____

_____

_____

_____

_____

_____

_____

_____

_____

_____

_____

- *David Goldberg*

Date:_____

"The abundant life forgets itself and fills its heart, time, and will with others."

- Brent Goddard

Date:_____

"Abundance is the physical manifestation
of our soul's true destiny."

_____
_____
_____
_____
_____
_____
_____
_____
_____
_____
_____
_____
_____
_____
_____
_____
_____
_____

- Marlaina Williams

*"Three keys to success: chasing your passion, carving your niche, and crucial financial insights."*

_____

_____

_____

_____

_____

_____

_____

_____

_____

_____

_____

_____

_____

_____

_____

_____

_____

_____

*- Nancy Sievert*

Date:_____

"Life simplified is power multiplied."

- Emmeline Saavedra

*"My photos are my transport to my best moments!"*

*- Geri Geasland*

Date:_____

"Abundance isn't something to chase; it is an experience to embrace. When I align with my soul, I open the door to an enchanted life of true abundance."

- Susan Kerby

Date:_____

*"Perseverance is life, determination
is fuel, and victory is our goal.
Let's go and get it!"*

349

- Roy Moore

Date:_____

"For one to live an abundant life, one must
be grateful."

_____

_____

_____

_____

_____

_____

_____

_____

_____

_____

_____

_____

_____

_____

_____

_____

_____

_____

- Carrie Van Amburgh

*Almost every part of the sunflower is edible, including seeds, petals, and even the stalks when prepared properly.*

-The Garden Fix

**Appreciation Is The Mother Of Abundance When You Count Your Blessings, The Number Becomes Infinite.**

-SueZee Finley

Date:_____

"Using the abundance, gratitude, and
emotions we have within us will create
durable relationships."

_____

_____

_____

_____

_____

_____

_____

_____

_____

_____

_____

_____

_____

_____

_____

_____

- Marc Beilin

*"Being thankful is a choice that will produce fruits like transformation."*

353

"Be genuinely grateful for all that you have at the moment, and you will hold the key to unlocking the door to all that you can imagine having."

- Leslie Kuntz

Date:_____

*"Make your life a beautiful story!
It is your birthright to create a life
you truly love!"*

*- Beth Robins*

Date:_____

"A great idea means nothing
without execution."

_____
_____
_____
_____
_____
_____
_____
_____
_____
_____
_____
_____
_____
_____
_____
_____
_____

- Britton Murrey

"At the moment you think that you have lost everything, pause and remind yourself that you will always have everything you need and more!"

- Karen Clark-Reddon

Date:_____

"*Abundance leads you to limitless possibilities that align with your mindset from endless gifts from the universe.*"

_____
_____
_____
_____
_____
_____
_____
_____
_____
_____
_____
_____
_____
_____
_____
_____
_____

- Tiffany Myles

"By feeling & rehearsing abundance, you align your energy with limitless possibilities, igniting the perfect vibe for your vision to shine in reality!"

- Angel Marie Monachelli

Date:_____

"Abundance is taking a leap of faith and following the call of the divine, for God is a God of abundance."

_____

_____

_____

_____

_____

_____

_____

_____

_____

_____

_____

_____

_____

_____

_____

_____

- Maureen Poirier

"It's not the fortune we accumulate but the love we share that defines us; every act of kindness creates ripples with the ability to transform lives."

- Alejandro Lopez

Date:_____

"Abundance thrives in energetic collaboration!"

_____

_____

_____

_____

_____

_____

_____

_____

_____

_____

_____

_____

_____

_____

_____

_____

_____

- Lucie Rosa-Stagi

Date:_____

"Any principle designed to create connection can also be used for manipulation—the difference lies in the sincere intentions of the heart."

363

— Christopher Arnold

Date:_____

"Abundance is an individual perspective each of us deems important, focusing upon our blessings and the many positive aspects of our lives."

_____
_____
_____
_____
_____
_____
_____
_____
_____
_____
_____
_____
_____
_____
_____
_____

- Mary Gilbert

"Fear is an option; courage is an option; quitting is an option; persevering is an option!"

- Ericka Avila

Date:_____

"*Abundance appears and fear disappears when you are grateful.*"

_____
_____
_____
_____
_____
_____
_____
_____
_____
_____
_____
_____
_____
_____
_____
_____

- *Joan Patterson*

Date:_____

"To let abundance flow, I learn to let go. Holding on won't make it stay. What's meant for me will find its way."

- Nicola Smith

Date:_____

"There's more to explore beyond
the clouds."

_____
_____
_____
_____
_____
_____
_____
_____
_____
_____
_____
_____
_____
_____
_____
_____

- Caydence Wong

"Peace of mind holds more value than any wealth; it's the foundation for true success and fulfillment."

_____

_____

_____

_____

_____

_____

_____

_____

_____

_____

_____

_____

_____

_____

_____

_____

_____

- Daniel Schneider

Date:_____

"The only way that you will fail is
if you give up; if you keep trying,
you will succeed."

- Phyl Franklin

Date:_____

*"The most valuable abundance assets one can hold are experiences."*

— Shawn Jones

Date:_____

"Abundance shows up in many forms throughout life. It has been said that abundance is a state of plenty. A supply of whatever is desired."

- Adrianne Size

"Our society doesn't fully comprehend the greatness of everyday life. We need artificial dates and holidays to celebrate what we should feel daily."

373

— Rutherford Pascal

Date:_____

*"When you let yourself open up, and you receive the true abundance of creativity, you feel the true power that is meant for you to see and make so."*

_____
_____
_____
_____
_____
_____
_____
_____
_____
_____
_____
_____
_____
_____
_____
_____
_____

*- Courtney Brown*

Date:_____

*"Abundance is like glasses: wear them to see the world clearly, or forget them and struggle through the day with vision loss."*

_____
_____
_____
_____
_____
_____
_____
_____
_____
_____
_____
_____
_____
_____
_____
_____
_____
_____

*- Stephen Turner*

Date:_____

"*How did we find abundance in our lives?*
*We had an estate sale!*"

_____
_____
_____
_____
_____
_____
_____
_____
_____
_____
_____
_____
_____
_____
_____
_____
_____
_____

- Allison Hammond

"Abundance and cannabis,
who would have thought?"

– Amethyst Kinney

# Check Out Our ART OF CONNECTION BOOK Series!

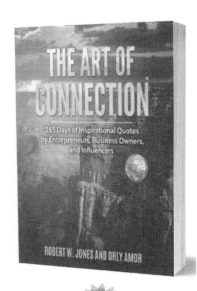

https://mybook.to/artofconnection

https://mybook.to/artofconnection2

https://mybook.to/artofconnection3

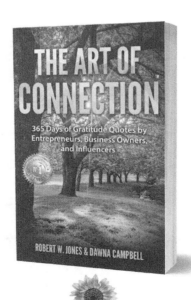

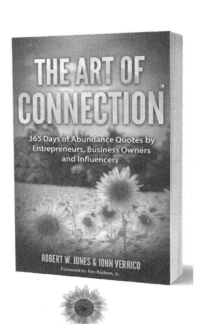

https://mybook.to/artofconnection4

https://mybook.to/artofconnection5

Made in the USA
Middletown, DE
21 February 2025

71604900R00210